HOW TO START, RUN AND GROW A NON-PROFITS ORGANIZATION

A Step-by-step Easy DIY Startup Guide to Run a Nonprofit Organization in 4-8 Weeks

Harry Martins

Copyright

All rights reserved.

No part of this work may be reproduced or transmitted in any form or by means, electronic or mechanical, including photography, recording, or by any information storage and retrieval system, without the prior permission of the copyright holder.

Table Of Contents

Demonstrating Value and Accountability 117

Part I: Building the Foundation

Discovering Your Cause

Starting a non-profit organization begins with a spark – a passion for a cause that ignites your desire to make a difference. This first section, "Discovering Your Cause," guides you through the crucial steps of identifying an unmet need, validating your idea, and crafting a powerful mission and values that will steer your organization toward success.

1. Identifying an Unmet Need

Begin by exploring the world around you. Look for gaps in your community, issues people face, or areas where existing solutions fall short. This could involve:

Personal experiences: Have you faced a challenge that others encounter too? Is there a lack of support in this area?

Community engagement: Talk to individuals and organizations working on related issues. Identify gaps in services or unmet needs.

Research and data: Explore reports, statistics, and studies to identify underserved populations or critical problems.

Remember, a strong non-profit fills a void, not duplicates existing efforts. Choose a niche where your organization can bring unique value and make a genuine impact.

2. Validating Your Idea:

Once you've identified a potential cause, take steps to confirm its relevance and viability. This involves:

Market research: Talk to potential beneficiaries, stakeholders, and experts in the field. Gauge their interest in your proposed solution.
Competitor analysis: Research existing organizations addressing similar issues. Identify their strengths and weaknesses to understand your potential positioning.
Feasibility assessment: Evaluate resource availability, funding potential, and operational challenges. Ensure your idea is sustainable and has a realistic pathway to success.

3. Defining Your Mission and Values:

With a validated need in focus, articulate your organization's purpose and guiding principles. Your mission statement should be a concise, clear declaration of your intended impact. Values define your organizational culture and the way you will operate.

Crafting a Mission Statement:

What problem are you solving?
Who are you helping?
What unique value do you offer?
Establishing Values:

What principles will guide your decision-making?
How will you interact with beneficiaries and stakeholders?
What commitment do you have to transparency and accountability?

A strong mission and values statement will attract supporters, guide your activities, and provide a foundation for lasting impact.

By diligently navigating these steps, you'll establish a solid foundation for your non-profit, ensuring you're addressing a genuine need with a viable and impactful solution. This will set the stage for the remaining sections of your book, guiding you through the process of launching, running, and growing your organization into a force for positive change.

Laying the Legal Groundwork:

Choosing the Right Non-Profit Structure:

Selecting the appropriate legal structure is the cornerstone of your non-profit's journey. It defines your operating framework, tax benefits, liability limitations, and overall governance. Navigating the choices can be daunting, but understanding the key distinctions will empower you to make an informed decision.

1. Unpacking the Options:

501(c)(3) Public Charity: The most common structure, offering comprehensive tax-exempt status for donations and income generated from charitable activities. Examples: educational institutions, homeless shelters, environmental organizations.

501(c)(4) Social Welfare Organization: Promotes social welfare but cannot engage in direct lobbying or political campaigns. Often used by advocacy groups and labor unions.

501(c)(5) Labor Organizations: Promotes the interests of workers and their families. Primarily used by unions and employee groups.

Unincorporated Association: A simpler setup, often suitable for small, informal groups conducting limited activities. Offers less legal and financial protection than incorporated structures.

Fiscal Sponsorship: Partnering with an established 501(c)(3) to leverage their tax-exempt status. Suitable for new organizations or those with limited fundraising capacity.

Each structure has unique eligibility requirements, governance principles, and limitations. Consider your mission, funding goals, intended activities, and risk tolerance to guide your selection.

Deep Dive into Incorporation:

Once you've chosen your structure, consider incorporating your non-profit. This provides several advantages:

Limited Liability: Protects board members and volunteers from personal liability for organizational debts or legal obligations.

Credibility and Trust: Enhances professional image, facilitates grant applications, and inspires donor confidence.

Fundraising Opportunities: Enables access to certain funding sources and simplifies financial management.

Incorporation involves filing articles of incorporation with your state, establishing bylaws, and appointing a board of directors. Seek legal counsel to ensure a smooth and compliant process.

Navigating the Tax-Exempt Maze:

Obtaining tax-exempt status under your chosen 501(c) category unlocks significant financial benefits. This involves applying for a determination letter from the IRS. Be prepared to submit detailed documentation outlining your mission, activities, governance structure, and financial projections.

Federal Tax Exemption: Donations to your organization are tax-deductible for donors, and your organization is exempt from most federal income taxes.

State and Local Tax Benefits: May benefit from exemptions on property taxes, sales taxes, and other levies.

Consulting with a tax professional familiar with non-profit regulations will ensure a successful application and maximize your tax-exempt benefits.

Choosing the right legal structure, incorporating your organization, and securing tax-exempt status are critical steps in establishing a strong foundation for your non-profit. By carefully considering your options and navigating the legalities with informed guidance, you can set your organization on a path to sustainable success and impactful change.

-

Assembling Your Team:

Building a Strong Board of Directors

The board of directors plays a pivotal role in the success and governance of any organization. Building a strong board requires careful consideration and strategic planning. The first step is identifying individuals with diverse skills, expertise, and a genuine passion for the organization's mission.

Diversity in backgrounds, experiences, and perspectives ensures a well-rounded board capable of making informed decisions. It's essential to recruit individuals with a mix of skills such as financial acumen, legal expertise, industry knowledge, and leadership experience. Additionally, potential board members should align with the organization's values and be committed to its long-term goals.

Once potential candidates are identified, a thorough vetting process should take place. This may include interviews, reference checks, and assessing candidates' previous experiences in similar roles. Effective communication and transparency about the organization's expectations and challenges are crucial during the recruitment process.

After assembling the board, fostering a culture of collaboration and open communication is vital. Regular board meetings, training sessions, and team-building activities contribute to a cohesive and effective board. Clearly defined expectations, term limits, and mechanisms for evaluating board performance should also be established to ensure accountability and continuous improvement.

Recruiting Key Staff and Volunteers

Recruiting key staff and volunteers is another critical aspect of organizational success. Identifying individuals who align with the organization's mission and values is key. Job descriptions should be well-crafted to attract candidates who not only have the necessary skills but also share a passion for the organization's goals.

For key staff positions, a rigorous hiring process should be implemented, including multiple rounds of interviews, skills assessments, and reference checks. Offering competitive compensation and benefits is essential to attract top talent. Additionally, providing opportunities for professional development and growth within the organization enhances retention.

Volunteers, who often serve as the backbone of many organizations, should be recruited strategically. Clearly communicate the impact of their contributions and recognize their efforts regularly. Creating a positive and inclusive volunteer culture fosters long-term commitment and enthusiasm.

Defining Roles and Responsibilities

Once the board, staff, and volunteers are in place, defining clear roles and responsibilities is essential for efficient operations. A well-structured organizational chart can visually depict reporting relationships and help prevent confusion. Each role should have a detailed job description outlining specific duties, expectations, and performance metrics.

Regular communication channels and feedback mechanisms should be established to ensure that everyone understands their responsibilities and can address any challenges or concerns. Training programs, workshops, and ongoing professional development opportunities can further enhance the skills and capabilities of the team.

Additionally, periodic reviews of roles and responsibilities allow for adjustments as the organization evolves. Flexibility is key to adapting to changing circumstances and leveraging the strengths of each team member.

In conclusion, building a strong board of directors, recruiting key staff and volunteers, and defining clear roles and responsibilities are interlinked components of effective organizational management. Strategic planning, thorough vetting processes, and ongoing communication contribute to the development of a capable and motivated team dedicated to achieving the organization's mission.

Developing Your Operating Framework:

Writing Bylaws and Conflict of Interest Policies

Bylaws serve as the foundation of an organization, providing a framework for its structure and operations. Crafting comprehensive bylaws is crucial for establishing clear guidelines on governance, decision-making processes, and member rights. The document typically includes information on the organization's purpose, membership criteria, board structure, meeting procedures, and procedures for amending the bylaws.

A Conflict of Interest Policy is an integral component of bylaws. This policy outlines the steps to identify, disclose, and manage conflicts that may arise among board members, staff, and volunteers. It ensures transparency, accountability, and the organization's commitment to ethical conduct. The policy typically requires individuals to disclose potential conflicts and abstain from voting on matters where they have a personal interest.

When drafting these documents, it is essential to involve legal expertise to ensure compliance with applicable laws and regulations. The bylaws and conflict of interest policies should reflect the organization's values, foster trust, and provide a solid framework for ethical decision-making.

Establishing Financial Management Systems

Sound financial management is the lifeblood of any successful organization. Establishing robust financial management systems is critical for fiscal responsibility, transparency, and sustainability. This involves creating budgeting processes, accounting procedures, and financial reporting mechanisms.

Developing an annual budget involves projecting income and expenses, allocating resources strategically, and ensuring financial sustainability. Accurate record-keeping and regular financial reporting to the board and relevant stakeholders are essential for informed decision-making.

Implementing effective accounting procedures involves maintaining a chart of accounts, tracking expenses, and ensuring compliance with accounting standards. Employing qualified financial professionals or engaging external auditors can help ensure the accuracy and integrity of financial data.

Financial oversight by the board is crucial. Regular financial reviews, audits, and the establishment of an internal control system help prevent fraud and financial mismanagement. Transparency in financial matters builds trust among stakeholders and donors.

Creating Operational Protocols

Operational protocols encompass the day-to-day procedures and workflows that guide the organization's activities. These protocols cover a broad range of areas, including program management, human resources, communications, and risk management.

Program management protocols detail how projects and initiatives are planned, executed, and evaluated. This includes setting goals, defining roles and responsibilities, and establishing performance metrics. Clear protocols ensure efficiency, consistency, and the achievement of organizational objectives.

Human resources protocols cover recruitment, onboarding, performance evaluations, and conflict resolution. Clearly defined policies on employee conduct, benefits, and professional development contribute to a positive organizational culture.

Communications protocols outline how the organization interacts with internal and external stakeholders. This includes guidelines for public relations, social media usage, and crisis communication. Consistent and transparent communication enhances the organization's reputation and relationships.

Risk management protocols identify potential risks and outline strategies for mitigation. This includes contingency planning, compliance monitoring, and the establishment of reporting mechanisms for incidents or concerns.

In summary, writing bylaws and conflict of interest policies, establishing financial management systems, and creating operational protocols are integral steps in the effective management of an organization. These foundational elements contribute to transparency, accountability, and the overall success of the organization in fulfilling its mission.

Part II: Launching and Leading

Fundraising Essentials:

Identifying Funding Sources

Identifying diverse and sustainable funding sources is a crucial aspect of organizational sustainability. This process involves comprehensive research to pinpoint potential donors, grant opportunities, and other financial support avenues. Understanding the organization's mission, goals, and projects is fundamental to aligning with funding sources that share similar values and priorities.

Government grants, private foundations, corporate sponsorships, individual donations, and collaborative partnerships are common funding sources. Organizations should diversify their funding streams to reduce dependency on a single source, mitigating financial risks.

Researching government grants involves staying informed about available programs at local, state, and federal levels. Private foundations often have specific focus areas, and organizations must tailor their proposals to align with these priorities. Building relationships with corporations that support philanthropic initiatives can lead to sponsorships and donations.

Regularly updating a comprehensive database of potential funding sources facilitates strategic planning. This database should include deadlines, application requirements, and contact information. Collaborating with fundraising professionals, attending industry conferences, and leveraging online platforms can enhance the organization's ability to identify and access funding opportunities.

Crafting Grant Proposals and Appeals

Crafting compelling grant proposals and appeals is an art that combines storytelling, data, and a clear articulation of the organization's impact. Successful proposals are tailored to the specific requirements of each funding source and clearly demonstrate how the organization's activities align with the funder's mission.

A well-structured grant proposal typically includes an executive summary, a detailed description of the organization and its mission, a needs statement, program objectives and methods, an evaluation plan, a budget, and a sustainability plan. Each section should be concise, persuasive, and supported by evidence.

In addition to written proposals, organizations often need to create engaging visual materials, such as videos or presentations, to complement their appeals. These materials should highlight the organization's achievements, showcase the impact of its work, and evoke an emotional connection with potential donors.

When appealing to individual donors, personalized communication is key. Tailor appeals to resonate with the donor's interests and motivations.

Regularly updating donors on the organization's progress and expressing gratitude for their contributions helps build long-lasting relationships.

Building Donor Relationships

Building and maintaining strong donor relationships is crucial for sustained financial support. Effective donor engagement involves more than just asking for contributions—it requires ongoing communication, transparency, and appreciation for the donors' impact on the organization's mission.

Personalized communication is essential in donor relationship-building. Regular newsletters, updates, and personalized messages expressing gratitude help donors feel connected to the organization's work.

Donors appreciate knowing how their contributions make a difference, so sharing success stories and showcasing the impact of their support strengthens the relationship.

Engaging donors in the organization's activities goes beyond financial contributions. Inviting donors to events, providing opportunities for volunteer involvement, and acknowledging their expertise or connections contribute to a sense of belonging and investment.

Donor stewardship involves transparently communicating how funds are utilized, demonstrating fiscal responsibility, and providing regular financial reports. Addressing concerns and inquiries promptly fosters trust and demonstrates the organization's commitment to accountability.

Building a donor recognition program acknowledges and honors the contributions of different donor levels. This could include naming opportunities, exclusive events, or other perks that show appreciation for the varying levels of support.

In conclusion, identifying diverse funding sources, crafting compelling grant proposals and appeals, and building strong donor relationships are integral components of a successful fundraising strategy. A well-rounded approach that combines research, communication, and appreciation contributes to the financial health and sustainability of the organization.

Program Design and Implementation:

Mapping Goals and Strategies

Mapping out clear and achievable goals is the first step in steering an organization towards success. This involves a thorough assessment of the organization's mission, vision, and values, followed by the identification of specific, measurable, achievable, relevant, and time-bound (SMART) goals. Goals should align with the organization's overall purpose and provide a roadmap for future initiatives.

Strategies, on the other hand, outline the approaches and plans for achieving these goals. Effective strategic planning involves assessing the internal and external environment, understanding potential challenges, and leveraging opportunities. Organizations often conduct SWOT (Strengths, Weaknesses, Opportunities, Threats) analyses to inform their strategies. Collaboration among key stakeholders, including board members, staff, and relevant community partners, ensures a comprehensive and well-informed strategic plan.

A clear roadmap with defined goals and strategies serves as a guide for decision-making, resource allocation, and organizational growth. Regular reviews and updates to the plan are essential to adapt to changing circumstances and ensure continued alignment with the organization's mission.

Developing Effective Programs and Services

Once goals and strategies are established, developing effective programs and services is the practical manifestation of the organization's mission. Programs and services should directly contribute to achieving the identified goals and align with the needs of the target audience or community.

Program development involves a systematic process that includes needs assessments, stakeholder input, program design, implementation plans, and evaluation mechanisms. Organizations should consider the scalability and sustainability of their programs, ensuring they can adapt to evolving circumstances and address emerging needs.

Engaging with the community and beneficiaries is critical during program development. Collecting feedback and incorporating the perspectives of those directly impacted ensures that programs are responsive to real needs and contribute to positive outcomes. Collaboration with other organizations, leveraging community resources, and fostering partnerships enhance program effectiveness.

Program evaluation is an ongoing process that measures the impact and effectiveness of programs. This includes assessing whether the intended outcomes are being achieved and if adjustments are needed. Evaluation data provides valuable insights for organizational learning and continuous improvement.

Measuring Impact and Evaluation

Measuring impact and evaluation are integral components of a results-oriented organization. Impact measurement goes beyond simple output metrics and seeks to understand the broader changes or benefits resulting from the organization's programs and services.

Impact measurement involves defining key performance indicators (KPIs) that align with the organization's goals. These KPIs may include quantitative metrics (e.g., number of beneficiaries served, outcomes achieved) and qualitative indicators (e.g., stories of change, community testimonials). Regular data collection and analysis provide a comprehensive understanding of the organization's impact over time.

Evaluation processes should be tailored to each program or service, considering the unique goals, target audience, and desired outcomes. Evaluation methods may include surveys, interviews, focus groups, and data analysis. Engaging external evaluators or experts in the field can provide an objective perspective and enhance the credibility of evaluation findings.

Sharing impact results with stakeholders, including donors, board members, staff, and the community, builds transparency and accountability. Positive impact stories and evidence of success contribute to the organization's reputation and help attract continued support.

In conclusion, mapping goals and strategies, developing effective programs and services, and measuring impact and evaluation are interconnected processes that form the backbone of successful organizational management. A thoughtful and dynamic approach to goal-setting, program development, and impact measurement contributes to an organization's ability to fulfill its mission and create lasting positive change.

Marketing and Advocacy:

Creating a Compelling Brand Identity

A compelling brand identity is the cornerstone of an organization's presence and reputation. It goes beyond a mere logo; it encompasses the values, personality, and visual elements that distinguish an organization from others. Developing a strong brand identity begins with a deep understanding of the organization's mission, vision, and values.

The process involves defining key brand elements such as the organization's name, logo, color palette, typography, and tone of voice. These elements should be carefully chosen to resonate with the target audience and convey the organization's unique personality. Consistency across all branding materials fosters recognition and trust among stakeholders.

Brand identity is not static; it evolves as the organization grows and adapts to changing contexts. Regularly revisiting and refining the brand identity ensures that it remains relevant and aligned with the organization's goals. Engaging with stakeholders, conducting market research, and staying attuned to industry trends are essential components of this iterative process.

A compelling brand identity serves as a powerful tool for building credibility, attracting support, and conveying the organization's impact. It establishes an emotional connection with the audience, fostering a sense of loyalty and affiliation.

Using Communication Channels Effectively

Effective communication is vital for conveying an organization's message and engaging with stakeholders. Utilizing various communication channels allows organizations to reach diverse audiences and share their stories in impactful ways. The key is understanding the strengths and nuances of each channel and tailoring the message accordingly.

Traditional channels such as press releases, print media, and direct mail still play a role, especially in reaching specific demographics. However, digital channels have become increasingly prominent. Websites, social media platforms, email newsletters, and podcasts offer dynamic and interactive ways to connect with audiences.

Crafting a coherent and compelling narrative is crucial across all communication channels. This narrative should highlight the organization's mission, achievements, and impact, fostering a consistent and recognizable brand image. Visual elements, such as images and graphics, should align with the brand identity to create a cohesive communication strategy.

Engagement is a two-way street, and organizations should encourage feedback and dialogue. Responding to comments on social media, hosting virtual town halls, and actively participating in relevant discussions contribute to a dynamic and responsive communication approach.

Engaging in Public Awareness and Advocacy

Public awareness and advocacy initiatives are instrumental in bringing attention to social issues, mobilizing support, and driving positive change. These efforts involve raising awareness about the organization's mission, educating the public on relevant issues, and advocating for policy changes that align with the organization's goals.

Public awareness campaigns often leverage a combination of media outreach, social media, events, and partnerships to reach a broad audience. These campaigns should be strategically planned to align with specific goals, whether it be fundraising, promoting a particular cause, or influencing public opinion.

Advocacy efforts aim to influence decision-makers and policymakers to create systemic change. This involves understanding the legislative landscape, building relationships with key stakeholders, and crafting persuasive arguments supported by data and evidence. Grassroots initiatives, such as petitions and community engagement events, can amplify advocacy efforts and demonstrate widespread support.

Collaboration with like-minded organizations and influencers can amplify the reach and impact of public awareness and advocacy campaigns. Building coalitions and alliances strengthens the collective voice advocating for change.

In conclusion, creating a compelling brand identity, using communication channels effectively, and engaging in public awareness and advocacy are interrelated strategies that contribute to an organization's visibility, influence, and impact. A thoughtful and integrated approach to branding and communication enhances the organization's ability to connect with stakeholders, inspire action, and drive positive change.

Leadership and Governance:

Cultivating Effective Board Relationships

The relationship between an organization's leadership and its board of directors is foundational to its success. Cultivating effective board relationships requires open communication, trust, and a shared commitment to the organization's mission and goals.

Regular communication is key to keeping the board informed and engaged. This involves not only reporting on organizational activities but also seeking input and feedback from board members. Scheduled board meetings, updates, and strategic planning sessions provide opportunities for meaningful dialogue and collaboration.

Building trust within the board is crucial for a harmonious working relationship. This trust is fostered through transparency, accountability, and demonstrating competence in organizational leadership. Board members should feel confident in the organization's direction and leadership team.

Clearly defined roles and responsibilities for both the executive leadership and the board contribute to effective governance. This includes understanding the board's role in strategic decision-making, fundraising, and oversight, as well as the executive leadership's responsibility for day-to-day operations. Regular training sessions and orientation for new board members ensure a shared understanding of expectations.

Recognizing and appreciating the diverse skills and experiences that board members bring to the table is essential. Board diversity in terms of background, expertise, and perspectives enriches the organization's decision-making processes. Creating a culture that values and respects this diversity enhances the overall effectiveness of the board.

In conclusion, cultivating effective board relationships requires ongoing effort to foster communication, build trust, clarify roles, and appreciate the diversity of perspectives within the board. A strong and collaborative relationship between the executive leadership and the board is fundamental to achieving organizational goals.

Managing Staff and Volunteers

Effective management of staff and volunteers is pivotal for the successful implementation of an organization's mission and programs. This involves creating a positive and inclusive organizational culture, providing adequate support and resources, and recognizing the contributions of team members.

Leadership sets the tone for organizational culture. A supportive and inclusive environment encourages staff and volunteers to actively engage in their roles. Clear communication of the organization's values and expectations contributes to a shared sense of purpose and commitment.

Recruitment and onboarding processes play a crucial role in integrating new staff and volunteers into the organization. Clearly defining roles, providing comprehensive training, and offering mentorship opportunities contribute to a smooth transition and set the stage for success.

Effective management includes ongoing professional development opportunities. Investing in the growth and skill enhancement of staff and volunteers not only benefits individuals but also strengthens the overall capacity of the organization. This may involve workshops, training sessions, or mentorship programs.

Recognition and appreciation are vital components of effective management. Acknowledging the efforts and achievements of staff and volunteers fosters a positive work environment and contributes to job satisfaction. This recognition can take various forms, including awards, public acknowledgment, or opportunities for advancement.

Conflict resolution mechanisms should be in place to address issues that may arise among staff or volunteers. A fair and transparent process for resolving disputes contributes to a healthy organizational culture and ensures that challenges are addressed constructively.

In conclusion, effective management of staff and volunteers involves creating a positive organizational culture, providing support and resources, offering ongoing development opportunities, and implementing fair conflict resolution mechanisms. A well-managed team is better positioned to achieve the organization's goals and contribute to its long-term success.

Ensuring Ethical and Transparent Practices

Ethical and transparent practices form the bedrock of a reputable and responsible organization. Upholding high ethical standards not only builds trust among stakeholders but also contributes to long-term sustainability and positive social impact. This commitment to ethics and transparency should permeate every aspect of an organization's operations.

1. Code of Ethics and Conduct:
Developing and implementing a comprehensive code of ethics and conduct is a fundamental step in

ensuring ethical practices. This document outlines the organization's values, principles, and guidelines for ethical behavior. It serves as a reference point for all stakeholders, including board members, staff, volunteers, and partners.

2. Transparent Governance:
Transparency in governance is crucial for building trust with stakeholders. Clearly defined governance structures, roles, and responsibilities should be accessible and understandable. Board meetings, decisions, and financial reports should be made available to relevant stakeholders, demonstrating a commitment to openness and accountability.

3. Financial Transparency:
Disclosing financial information is a key element of transparency.

Organizations should provide clear and accurate financial statements, including revenue, expenses, and allocation of funds. Regular financial audits by external professionals help ensure accuracy and adherence to financial best practices.

4. Stakeholder Engagement:
Engaging with stakeholders openly and inclusively contributes to ethical decision-making. This involves seeking input from various groups, including beneficiaries, donors, and community members. Listening to diverse perspectives ensures that the organization considers the impact of its actions on all stakeholders.

5. Conflict of Interest Policies:
Establishing and enforcing robust conflict of interest policies is essential to prevent any undue influence or bias. Board members, staff, and

volunteers should disclose any potential conflicts, and mechanisms should be in place to manage and mitigate these conflicts appropriately.

6. Whistleblower Protection:
Encouraging a culture where individuals feel safe reporting unethical practices is vital. Whistleblower protection policies should be in place to shield individuals who come forward with concerns. This promotes a culture of accountability and helps the organization address issues promptly.

7. Compliance with Laws and Regulations:
Adhering to local, national, and international laws and regulations is a fundamental aspect of ethical conduct. Organizations should stay informed about legal requirements relevant to their operations and

ensure strict compliance to avoid legal and reputational risks.

8. Social Responsibility:
Incorporating social responsibility into organizational practices goes beyond legal obligations. It involves considering the environmental, social, and economic impact of the organization's activities. Implementing sustainable practices and contributing positively to the community align with ethical standards.

9. Continuous Evaluation and Improvement:
Ethical practices are not static; they require continuous evaluation and improvement. Regularly reviewing and updating policies and procedures, seeking feedback from stakeholders, and learning from past experiences contribute to an evolving

commitment to ethics and transparency.

In conclusion, ensuring ethical and transparent practices is a multifaceted commitment that permeates the culture, governance, and operations of an organization. By upholding these principles, an organization not only builds trust but also contributes to the broader goal of creating a positive and responsible impact on society.

Part III: Growth and Sustainability

Strategic Planning and Expansion:

Setting SMART Goals and Objectives

Setting SMART goals and objectives is a strategic approach that ensures clarity, focus, and effectiveness in organizational planning. SMART stands for Specific, Measurable, Achievable, Relevant, and Time-bound, providing a structured framework for goal-setting.

1. Specific:

Goals should be well-defined and clear, leaving no room for ambiguity. A specific goal answers the questions: What needs to be accomplished? Why is it important? Who is involved? Where will it happen? This clarity guides the organization in a purposeful direction.

2. Measurable:
Measuring progress is essential to tracking success. Goals should include quantifiable indicators that allow for objective assessment. This involves defining metrics, milestones, or key performance indicators (KPIs) that indicate whether the goal has been achieved.

3. Achievable:
Setting realistic and attainable goals is crucial for maintaining motivation and preventing frustration. While goals should challenge the

organization, they should also be feasible given the available resources and constraints. This ensures that the organization sets itself up for success.

4. Relevant:
Goals should align with the organization's mission and strategic priorities. They need to be relevant to the overall vision, ensuring that efforts contribute to the organization's long-term success. Irrelevant goals can divert resources and energy away from strategic objectives.

5. Time-bound:
Setting a timeframe creates a sense of urgency and provides a deadline for achieving the goal. This helps prevent procrastination and encourages a focused and disciplined approach. Time-bound goals also facilitate

regular reviews and adjustments to stay on track.

Strategic planning often involves breaking down overarching goals into smaller, more manageable objectives. Regularly reviewing and revising these goals ensures that the organization remains adaptable and responsive to changing circumstances.

Diversifying Funding Streams

Diversifying funding streams is a crucial strategy for ensuring financial sustainability and resilience. Over-reliance on a single funding source can expose an organization to significant risks. Diversification involves seeking support from various channels, reducing dependence on any one donor or revenue stream.

1. Identify Potential Funding Sources:
Conduct thorough research to identify potential funding sources that align with the organization's mission and programs. This may include government grants, private foundations, corporate sponsorships, individual donors, and earned revenue streams.

2. Tailor Funding Proposals:
Crafting targeted and compelling funding proposals is essential for capturing the attention of different donors. Each proposal should be customized to meet the specific requirements and interests of the funding source. Clearly communicate how the organization's activities align with the donor's priorities.

3. Build Relationships:

Building strong relationships with donors and supporters is a continuous process. Regular communication, updates on achievements, and expressing gratitude for contributions contribute to a positive and lasting connection. Donors are more likely to continue their support when they feel engaged and informed.

4. Explore Earned Revenue Models:
In addition to traditional fundraising, organizations can explore sustainable business models that generate revenue. This may involve offering fee-based services, merchandise sales, or other income-generating activities. These models contribute to financial stability and reduce dependency on donations.

5. Collaborate and Network:

Collaborating with other organizations and networking within the community can open up new funding opportunities. Partnerships can lead to joint funding applications, shared resources, and increased visibility, enhancing the organization's overall fundraising capacity.

6. Plan for Contingencies:
Financial planning should include contingencies for potential shifts in funding. Having a diversified portfolio of funding sources provides a safety net in case one source becomes unavailable. This proactive approach prepares the organization for financial challenges.

7. Assess and Adjust:
Regularly assess the effectiveness of current fundraising strategies and the balance of funding sources. If certain

sources become unreliable or new opportunities arise, be prepared to adjust the fundraising strategy accordingly. Flexibility is key to long-term financial sustainability.

Scaling up Programs and Services

Scaling up programs and services is a strategic process of expanding the reach and impact of an organization's initiatives. This growth requires careful planning, resource allocation, and a focus on maintaining program quality.

1. Assess Readiness and Capacity:
Before scaling up, assess the organization's readiness and capacity. This involves evaluating existing infrastructure, human resources, financial stability, and the scalability of current programs. Ensure that the organization can effectively manage

expansion without compromising quality.

2. Set Clear Objectives:
Define clear and specific objectives for scaling up programs. These objectives should align with the organization's mission and strategic goals. Whether it's reaching a larger geographic area, serving more beneficiaries, or introducing new services, clarity in objectives guides the scaling process.

3. Develop a Scaling Plan:
Create a detailed scaling plan that outlines the steps, timelines, and resources required for expansion. This plan should address potential challenges and risks, and include mechanisms for monitoring and evaluating the impact of scaling on program outcomes.

4. Secure Funding:
Scaling up requires additional resources, including funding. Develop a comprehensive budget that accounts for increased operational costs, staff capacity, and any additional infrastructure needed. Seek funding from existing donors, explore new funding opportunities, and consider earned revenue models.

5. Build Partnerships:
Collaborate with other organizations, government agencies, or community partners to facilitate the scaling process. Partnerships can provide additional resources, expertise, and support, enhancing the organization's ability to reach broader audiences.

6. Implement Pilot Programs:
Before full-scale expansion, consider implementing pilot programs or phased approaches. This allows the

organization to test the scalability of the program, identify potential challenges, and make necessary adjustments before reaching a larger audience.

7. Monitor and Evaluate:
Implement robust monitoring and evaluation mechanisms to assess the impact of scaled-up programs. Collect data on key performance indicators, track outcomes, and solicit feedback from beneficiaries and stakeholders. This information informs ongoing improvements and ensures program effectiveness.

8. Learn from Experience:
Scaling up is a learning process. Regularly review the outcomes and experiences of scaled programs, identify lessons learned, and apply these insights to future scaling initiatives. Continuous improvement

based on real-world feedback contributes to the organization's overall effectiveness.

In conclusion, setting SMART goals and objectives, diversifying funding streams, and scaling up programs and services are interconnected strategies that contribute to the overall success and sustainability of an organization. Thoughtful planning, adaptability, and a focus on impact are essential elements of effective organizational management.

Building Resilience and Adaptability:

Managing Risk and Change

Effective organizational management involves navigating both internal and external factors, and managing risk and change is central to this process. Understanding the potential risks that may impact the organization allows for proactive measures and strategic decision-making.

1. Risk Assessment:
Conducting a thorough risk assessment involves identifying potential threats to the organization's goals and operations. This includes financial risks, operational risks, reputational risks, and external factors such as changes in regulations or market dynamics. Regular risk assessments help the organization

anticipate challenges and develop mitigation strategies.

2. Risk Mitigation Strategies:
Once risks are identified, organizations should develop and implement risk mitigation strategies. This may involve creating contingency plans, diversifying funding sources, obtaining insurance, or establishing internal controls. Effectively managing risks safeguards the organization's stability and enhances its ability to adapt to unforeseen challenges.

3. Change Management:
Change is inevitable, and organizations must be equipped to navigate and implement change effectively. This involves clear communication with stakeholders, outlining the reasons for the change, and addressing concerns.

Implementing change management methodologies ensures a smooth transition and minimizes resistance from staff and other stakeholders.

4. Flexibility and Adaptability:
Cultivating a culture of flexibility and adaptability is essential for managing risk and change. This involves fostering an environment where staff members are open to new ideas, willing to embrace change, and capable of adapting to evolving circumstances. A flexible organization is better positioned to respond to external challenges and capitalize on emerging opportunities.

5. Continuous Monitoring:
Risk management is an ongoing process that requires continuous monitoring of internal and external factors. Regularly reassessing the organizational landscape, staying

informed about industry trends, and evaluating the effectiveness of risk mitigation strategies contribute to a proactive and resilient organization.

6. Learning from Setbacks:
Inevitably, organizations may face setbacks or encounter unexpected challenges. The key is to view setbacks as learning opportunities. Conducting post-event evaluations, identifying areas for improvement, and integrating lessons learned into future strategies contribute to organizational resilience.

Embracing Innovation and Collaboration

Innovation and collaboration are fundamental drivers of organizational growth and adaptability. Embracing a culture that encourages creativity, experimentation, and collaboration fosters a dynamic and forward-thinking organization.

1. Encouraging Creativity:
Creating an environment that encourages creativity involves empowering staff to generate and explore new ideas. This may include setting aside time for brainstorming sessions, creating cross-functional teams, and recognizing and rewarding innovative contributions. Encouraging a culture of creativity leads to the development of novel solutions and approaches.

2. Embracing Technology:
Innovation often involves leveraging technology to enhance efficiency and effectiveness. Organizations should stay abreast of technological advancements relevant to their field and be willing to invest in and adopt new tools and systems that can streamline processes and improve outcomes.

3. Collaboration and Partnerships:
Collaboration with external entities, such as other organizations, academic institutions, or industry partners, can fuel innovation. Building strategic partnerships broadens the organization's network, brings in diverse perspectives, and facilitates the sharing of resources and expertise.

4. Cross-functional Teams:

Creating cross-functional teams allows individuals from different departments or areas of expertise to collaborate on projects. This interdisciplinary approach fosters a holistic understanding of challenges and encourages innovative solutions that draw on diverse skills and perspectives.

5. Learning from Failure:

Innovation inherently involves a degree of experimentation, and not every initiative will succeed. Embracing a culture that views failure as a learning opportunity encourages risk-taking and resilience. Analyzing the reasons for failure and applying those insights to future endeavors contribute to ongoing innovation.

Cultivating a Culture of Learning and Growth

A culture of learning and growth is a cornerstone of organizational development. This involves creating an environment where continuous learning is valued, employees are empowered to enhance their skills, and the organization as a whole is committed to adaptability and improvement.

1. Professional Development Opportunities:
Providing professional development opportunities for staff is essential for fostering a culture of learning. This may include training sessions, workshops, conferences, and access to educational resources. Investing in the growth of employees not only enhances their individual capabilities

but also contributes to the overall competency of the organization.

2. Leadership Development:

Leadership plays a crucial role in cultivating a culture of learning. Developing leadership programs that focus on skills such as communication, decision-making, and adaptability creates a cadre of leaders who can guide the organization through change and innovation.

3. Continuous Feedback:

Implementing a system of continuous feedback contributes to individual and organizational growth. Regular performance evaluations, constructive feedback, and open communication channels create a culture where learning is a two-way process. This feedback loop supports ongoing improvement and development.

4. Knowledge Sharing:
Encouraging knowledge sharing among staff members promotes a collaborative learning environment. Establishing platforms for sharing best practices, lessons learned, and innovative ideas enables the organization to benefit from the collective knowledge and experiences of its workforce.

5. Adaptability to Change:
A culture of learning and growth is closely tied to an organization's adaptability to change. Emphasizing the importance of adaptability, resilience, and a willingness to embrace new ideas creates a workforce that is better equipped to navigate challenges and capitalize on opportunities.

6. Recognition of Achievements:
Recognizing and celebrating individual and team achievements fosters a positive learning culture. Acknowledging milestones, successful projects, and personal development accomplishments reinforces the organization's commitment to growth and creates a sense of pride among staff members.

7. Continuous Improvement Initiatives:
Establishing processes for continuous improvement involves regularly assessing organizational practices, identifying areas for enhancement, and implementing strategic changes. This commitment to ongoing improvement ensures that the organization remains agile and responsive to evolving needs.

In conclusion, effective organizational management requires a comprehensive approach to managing risk and change, embracing innovation and collaboration, and cultivating a culture of learning and growth. These interrelated strategies contribute to an organization's resilience, adaptability, and long-term success in a dynamic and evolving landscape.

Advocacy and Policy Influence:

Identifying Policy Levers for Change

Identifying policy levers for change is a strategic approach that empowers organizations to influence and shape the policies that impact their mission and goals. Policymaking occurs at various levels, including local, regional, and national, and understanding the levers that can drive change is crucial for effective advocacy.

1. Policy Analysis:
Organizations must conduct thorough policy analysis to identify areas where change is needed. This involves assessing existing policies,

understanding their implications, and identifying gaps or areas for improvement. Analyzing the policy landscape allows organizations to pinpoint specific issues that align with their mission.

2. Stakeholder Mapping:
Identifying key stakeholders involved in policymaking is essential. This includes government officials, lawmakers, regulatory bodies, and advocacy groups. Understanding the interests and influence of these stakeholders helps organizations strategically target their advocacy efforts.

3. Legislative Advocacy:
Engaging in legislative advocacy involves actively participating in the policymaking process. This may include providing expert testimony, submitting written comments on

proposed legislation, and building relationships with lawmakers. Organizations can leverage their expertise and data to inform and shape policy discussions.

4. Grassroots Advocacy:
Mobilizing grassroots support is a powerful policy lever. Engaging the community, beneficiaries, and supporters in advocacy efforts amplifies the organization's voice. This may involve organizing grassroots campaigns, petitions, and community forums to raise awareness and garner public support for specific policy changes.

5. Coalition Building:
Building coalitions with like-minded organizations strengthens advocacy efforts. Collaborating with other entities that share common goals amplifies the collective impact.

Coalitions provide a unified voice, share resources, and present a coordinated front to policymakers.

6. Data and Research:
Utilizing data and research is a persuasive tool in advocating for policy change. Organizations should invest in robust data collection and research efforts to support their arguments. Well-documented evidence enhances the credibility of the organization's advocacy and provides a compelling case for policy reforms.

7. Media Advocacy:
Engaging with the media is a crucial aspect of influencing public opinion and policymakers. Organizations should develop media strategies that include press releases, op-eds, and interviews to disseminate

information, shape narratives, and garner support for policy changes.

8. Policy Education:
Educating policymakers and the public about the impact of specific policies is vital. This involves creating informational materials, conducting awareness campaigns, and providing resources that explain the need for change. Informed policymakers are more likely to support and champion policy reforms.

Engaging in Grassroots Mobilization

Grassroots mobilization is a bottom-up approach to creating social and political change, mobilizing individuals at the community level to collectively advocate for a shared cause. This approach empowers ordinary citizens to become active participants in the change process.

1. Community Organizing:
Community organizing is at the heart of grassroots mobilization. It involves building relationships within communities, identifying local leaders, and fostering a sense of collective ownership and responsibility. Organizations should empower community members to identify and address issues that matter to them.

2. Empowering Local Leaders:
Identifying and empowering local leaders is crucial for sustainable grassroots mobilization. These leaders, often from within the community, play a central role in mobilizing their peers, disseminating information, and organizing community actions. Training and supporting these leaders enhance their effectiveness.

3. Door-to-Door Campaigns:
Conducting door-to-door campaigns is an effective way to engage directly with community members. This approach allows organizations to listen to individual concerns, provide information, and build relationships. Door-to-door campaigns create a personal connection, fostering trust and buy-in for grassroots initiatives.

4. Use of Technology:
Leveraging technology is a modern approach to grassroots mobilization. Social media, mobile apps, and online platforms provide efficient tools for reaching and engaging a wide audience. Organizations should utilize these technologies to share information, organize events, and mobilize supporters.

5. Workshops and Training:
Organizing workshops and training sessions within communities provides opportunities for skill-building and knowledge-sharing. These sessions can focus on advocacy, leadership development, and organizing strategies. Empowering community members with the necessary skills enhances the sustainability of grassroots initiatives.

6. Collaborative Decision-Making:
Grassroots mobilization thrives on collaborative decision-making. Involving community members in the decision-making process ensures that initiatives reflect their needs and aspirations. Creating spaces for dialogue and consensus-building fosters a sense of shared ownership and commitment.

7. Artistic and Cultural Engagement:
Engaging with the arts and culture can be a powerful tool for grassroots mobilization. Cultural events, artistic expressions, and storytelling resonate deeply with communities. Incorporating these elements into mobilization efforts helps connect with people on an emotional level, fostering a sense of identity and shared purpose.

8. Community Events and Actions: Organizing community events and actions creates opportunities for collective expression. Rallies, town hall meetings, and public demonstrations draw attention to specific issues, generate public awareness, and demonstrate the strength of community support for a cause.

Collaborating with Partners and Stakeholders

Collaboration with partners and stakeholders is a cornerstone of effective organizational management. Engaging with external entities, including other organizations, government agencies, businesses, and community groups, amplifies the impact of initiatives and creates a network of support.

1. Identifying Key Stakeholders:
Identifying and understanding key stakeholders is a foundational step in collaboration. This involves mapping out individuals, organizations, and groups that have a vested interest in or are affected by the organization's mission and activities. Key stakeholders may include beneficiaries, donors, government agencies, and community leaders.

2. Building Strategic Partnerships:
Strategic partnerships involve intentional collaborations

Assessing Impact and Measuring Success:

Defining Impact Metrics and Indicators

Defining impact metrics and indicators is a critical aspect of effective organizational management, providing a framework for measuring the outcomes and success of programs and initiatives. Impact metrics are specific, quantifiable measures that gauge the extent to which an organization is achieving its intended goals and creating positive change.

1. Clarity in Objectives:
Before defining impact metrics, organizations must have clear and well-defined objectives. These objectives serve as the foundation for identifying the metrics that will

effectively measure progress toward desired outcomes. Clarity in objectives ensures that the chosen metrics align with the organization's mission and strategic goals.

2. SMART Criteria:
Impact metrics should adhere to the SMART criteria—Specific, Measurable, Achievable, Relevant, and Time-bound. Each metric should be clearly defined, quantifiable, realistic to measure, directly related to the intended impact, and associated with a specific timeframe for assessment.

3. Stakeholder Involvement:
Involving stakeholders in the process of defining impact metrics enhances the relevance and credibility of the measurements. Engaging beneficiaries, staff, donors, and other relevant parties ensures that a

diversity of perspectives is considered, leading to a more comprehensive set of metrics that accurately reflects the organization's impact.

4. Balanced Approach:
A balanced approach to impact metrics considers both quantitative and qualitative indicators. While quantitative data provides numerical measurements, qualitative insights offer a deeper understanding of the impact, including beneficiaries' stories, changes in behavior, and qualitative assessments of program success.

5. Long-Term and Short-Term Indicators:
Impact metrics should encompass both long-term and short-term indicators. Short-term indicators measure immediate outputs and

changes, while long-term indicators capture sustained impact over time. This dual focus allows organizations to assess the effectiveness of their programs at different stages.

6. Continuous Review and Adaptation:
Impact metrics are not static and should be subject to continuous review and adaptation. As organizational goals evolve and external factors change, it is essential to reassess and update impact metrics to ensure their ongoing relevance and effectiveness.

Conducting Program Evaluations

Program evaluations are systematic processes designed to assess the effectiveness, efficiency, and relevance of an organization's programs. These evaluations provide valuable insights that inform decision-making, improve program delivery, and demonstrate accountability to stakeholders.

1. Evaluation Framework:
Establishing a clear evaluation framework is the foundation of a successful program evaluation. This framework outlines the objectives, scope, methodology, and timeline of the evaluation. It serves as a roadmap for the evaluation process and ensures consistency and rigor in data collection and analysis.

2. Define Evaluation Questions:
Clearly defining evaluation questions guides the assessment process. These questions should align with the organization's goals and address specific aspects of the program's impact, implementation, and relevance. Common evaluation

questions may focus on program effectiveness, efficiency, participant satisfaction, and overall impact.

3. Mixed-Methods Approach:
Utilizing a mixed-methods approach combines quantitative and qualitative data collection and analysis methods. Surveys, interviews, focus groups, and statistical analyses provide a comprehensive understanding of the program's outcomes and allow for triangulation of data to enhance the validity and reliability of findings.

4. Engage External Evaluators:
In some cases, engaging external evaluators or third-party organizations can enhance the objectivity and credibility of the evaluation process. External evaluators bring an independent perspective and may have specialized expertise in evaluation

methodologies, ensuring a thorough and unbiased assessment.

5. Continuous Improvement:
Program evaluations should not be viewed as one-time events but as opportunities for continuous improvement. Organizations should use evaluation findings to identify strengths, weaknesses, and areas for enhancement. This iterative process contributes to organizational learning and programmatic refinement.

6. Transparent Communication:
Transparent communication throughout the evaluation process is crucial. This includes informing stakeholders about the purpose and scope of the evaluation, providing regular updates on progress, and sharing the findings and recommendations in a clear and accessible manner. Transparent

communication builds trust and accountability.

Demonstrating Value and Accountability

Demonstrating value and accountability is integral to maintaining the trust of stakeholders, including donors, beneficiaries, and the wider community. Clear communication of an organization's impact, achievements, and responsible use of resources enhances its credibility and fosters ongoing support.

1. Impact Reporting:
Regular and transparent reporting on the impact of programs is essential. This involves sharing quantifiable data, success stories, and testimonials that highlight the positive changes brought about by the organization's

initiatives. Impact reports should align with defined impact metrics and indicators.

2. Financial Accountability:
Maintaining financial accountability is a cornerstone of organizational transparency. Organizations should adhere to sound financial management practices, conduct regular audits, and clearly communicate financial information to stakeholders. Demonstrating responsible stewardship of resources enhances donor confidence and support.

3. Compliance with Standards:
Adhering to industry standards and ethical guidelines enhances an organization's credibility. This includes compliance with legal requirements, adherence to best practices in program delivery, and

alignment with relevant industry standards. Organizations may consider obtaining certifications or accreditations to demonstrate their commitment to quality and accountability.

4. Stakeholder Engagement:
Engaging with stakeholders actively involves them in the organization's decision-making processes, communicates a commitment to transparency, and allows for feedback and input. Regular communication with beneficiaries, donors, and the community fosters a sense of inclusion and accountability.

5. Evaluation Findings:
Sharing the findings of program evaluations, both successes and areas for improvement, is a powerful way to demonstrate accountability. Transparently presenting evaluation

results, along with action plans for addressing identified challenges, shows a commitment to learning, adaptation, and continuous improvement.

6. Open Communication Channels:
Maintaining open communication channels with stakeholders fosters an environment of trust and accountability. Providing opportunities for stakeholders to ask questions, express concerns, and engage in dialogue contributes to a transparent and responsive organizational culture.

7. Learning from Mistakes:
Acknowledging and learning from mistakes is a key aspect of accountability. Organizations should be transparent about challenges or setbacks, communicate the steps taken to address them, and share the

lessons learned. This approach demonstrates humility, a commitment to improvement, and a focus on organizational growth.

In conclusion, defining impact metrics and indicators, conducting program evaluations, and demonstrating value and accountability are interconnected processes that contribute to effective organizational management. These practices not only enhance.